WIND POWER
Is It Reliable?

JIM PIPE

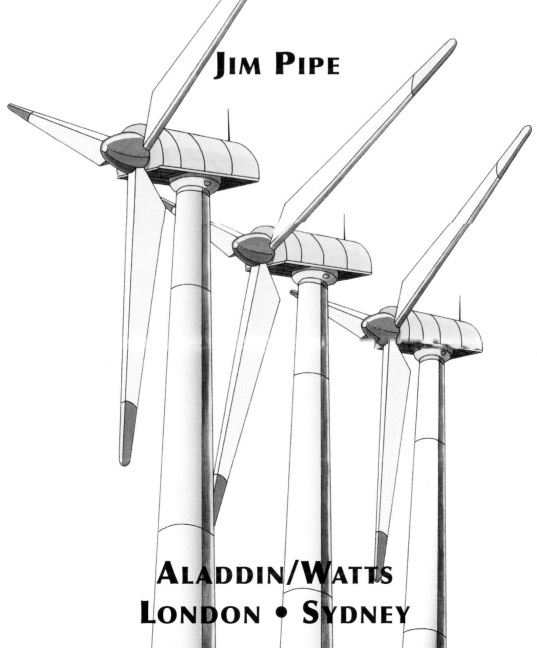

ALADDIN/WATTS
LONDON • SYDNEY

Contents

Why Wind?   4

What Is Wind Energy?   6

Capturing the Wind   8

Wind Turbines   10

Wind Farms   12

Local Wind Power   14

Who Uses Wind Power?   16

A Green Energy Source   18

What's the Catch?   20

Can Wind Work?   22

Future Trends   24

Hot Off the Press   26

How Wind Compares   28

Glossary and Resources (including World Wind Map)   30

Index   32

© Aladdin Books Ltd 2010

Designed and produced by
Aladdin Books Ltd
PO Box 53987
London SW15 2SF

First published in 2010
by Franklin Watts
338 Euston Road
London NW1 3BH

Franklin Watts Australia
Level 17/207 Kent Street
Sydney NSW 2000

Franklin Watts is a division of
Hachette Children's Books,
an Hachette UK company.
www.hachette.co.uk

All rights reserved
Printed in Malaysia

Scientific consultant: Rob Bowden

A catalogue record for
this book is available
from the British Library.

Dewey Classification:
333.9'2

ISBN 978 07496 9078 6

What's the Issue?

Wind power has been used for centuries to grind grain or pump water. Today, wind turbines can capture the energy of moving air and turn this into electricity. They could help to provide a solution to the world's energy problems. Most of our energy comes from fossil fuels such as oil, gas and coal. However, burning fossil fuels releases gases that add to global warming, as well as polluting the air. The challenge is to find a reliable alternative without adding to our environmental problems.

Along with other renewable energies such as solar and water power, wind turbines can provide power without polluting the atmosphere. But the wind is not reliable – some days it does not blow. It also takes thousands of turbines to produce the same energy as a power station.

Wind pumps

use wind energy to pump water from deep underground up to the surface.

Wind turbines

convert wind energy to electricity. These turbines are in Helanshan, China.

Why Wind?

Dutch Windmill

Wind energy was used for hundreds of years to pump water or "mill" (grind) grain, from Persia (now Iran) and the Netherlands to the United States. Today, several hundred thousand windmills are still used around the world to pump water.

Modern windmills – called wind turbines – can capture the wind's energy and convert it into electricity. This wind energy can provide the power to light and heat our homes, offices and factories, and even to power electric cars.

◖ Windmills

Around the 7th century AD, the first windmills were built in Persia (now Iran) with their sails in a horizontal position. By the time windmills arrived in Europe, around 1180, they had their sails in the upright position we are used to seeing on windmills in Holland and the UK. In 1745, English engineer Edmund Lee invented the fantail, which automatically turned the windmill to face the wind.

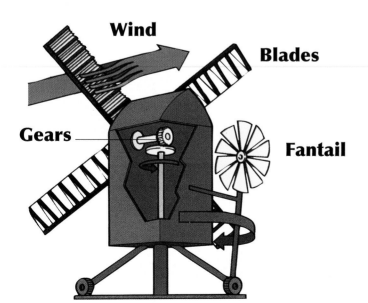

Wind

Blades

Gears

Fantail

◖ How a Windmill Works

1 The wind blows, hitting the fantail.
2 The fantail is pushed around, turning the windmill's blades towards the wind.
3 The wind turns the blades.
4 The blades are connected by a shaft to gears inside the windmill, driving the machinery that grinds the corn.
5 If the wind changes direction, the fantail turns the mill around until the wind is pushing the blades again.

WIND POWER: For

• It is a clean alternative to coal and gas. Wind turbines produce no waste and, once they are built, create no greenhouse gases.
• Wind is renewable – it can be used again and again and will never run out, unlike today's biggest sources of energy: oil, gas and coal.
• Wind farms need no fuel. Once the turbines have been built, the wind is free.
• The land around can still be farmed.
• Wind turbines are a good way to supply electricity to remote areas.
• Wind energy is increasingly cheap.

WIND POWER: Against

• The wind is unpredictable – some days have no wind, others have too much wind.
• Suitable areas for wind farms are often near the coast, where land is expensive.
• Some people feel that wind turbines look ugly and spoil the countryside.
• Turbines can sometimes kill birds.
• Turbines can affect radar systems and television reception if you live nearby.
• Turbines can be noisy. Older wind generators can make a constant, low, "swooshing" noise day and night, which can drive people mad! However, modern turbines are usually much quieter.

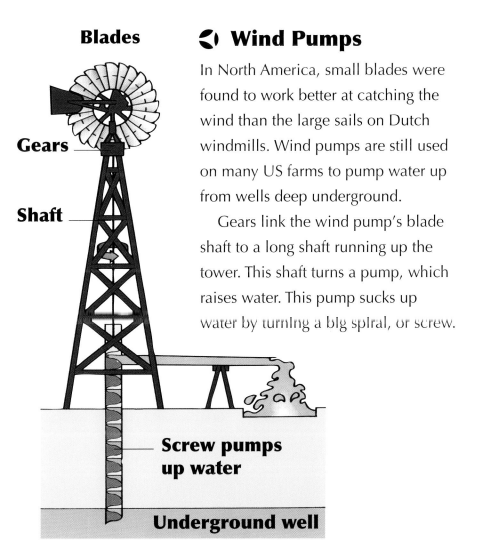

Blades

Gears

Shaft

Screw pumps up water

Underground well

◁ Wind Pumps

In North America, small blades were found to work better at catching the wind than the large sails on Dutch windmills. Wind pumps are still used on many US farms to pump water up from wells deep underground.

Gears link the wind pump's blade shaft to a long shaft running up the tower. This shaft turns a pump, which raises water. This pump sucks up water by turning a big spiral, or screw.

ENERGY FACTS: A Short History of Wind Turbines

1887 US Inventor Charles F. Brush builds the first wind turbine to generate electricity. It has an iron tower and a 17-metre-wide wheel.
1899 Danish inventor Poul la Cour improves the design with curved blades.
1918 Wind turbines provide 3 per cent of electricity in Denmark.
1930s Small wind machines are built to charge batteries.
1979 Modern wind power industry starts as many wind turbines built in Denmark.
2000s Wind power is fastest growing renewable energy technology in the world.

What Is Wind Energy

Wind is air on the move from one place to another. It can move at different speeds and strengths. This movement makes clouds drift across the sky and changes the weather. People have harnessed the power of the wind for thousands of years, powering mills and pumps, sailing boats, kites – and windsurfers. Modern wind turbines use the same power to generate electricity.

What Is Wind?

Wind is a form of solar power. As the Sun heats the surface of our planet, some places get hotter than others, thanks to the tilt of the Earth. Warm air is light and rises, while cold air is heavier and sinks. This movement creates wind currents high up in the air, which is the turbulence you feel in an aeroplane.

The high-flying air currents are part of a giant weather machine that stretches around the whole planet. It's driven by the Sun's energy and the oceans, which store heat like a giant hot water bottle. We feel the moving air currents on the ground, too – as wind.

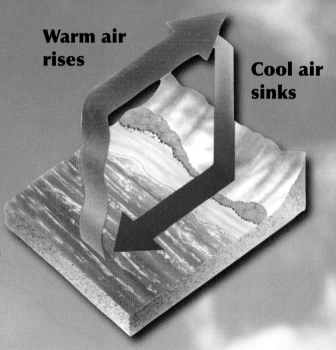

Warm air rises

Cool air sinks

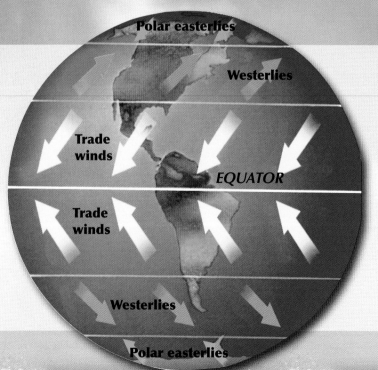

Polar easterlies

Westerlies

Trade winds

Trade winds

EQUATOR

Westerlies

Polar easterlies

World Winds

There is an overall pattern to the world's winds, caused by the spin of the Earth. This rotation makes the winds blowing towards the equator move from east to west. These are often called the trade winds as they were once used by merchant ships. Winds further from the equator, the Westerlies, blow the other way.

The global pattern of winds affects the world's climate, including violent storms such as hurricanes and typhoons.

Windsurfer
A strong wind has lifted this windsurfer high above the surface of the water.

Wind Power
The same wind energy that pushes a boat through the water turns the blades of a turbine.

High Winds

Most of the energy stored in atmospheric wind movements is found at high altitudes. Here, winds known as the jetstream blow continuously at speeds of over 160 km/h (100 mph).

Wind is generally much stronger high up in the air than close to the ground. That's why a kite flies better as it climbs, and why wind turbines are often built on hills or above cliffs.

Catching the Wind

Around 6,000 years ago, the ancient Egyptians were among the first people to use sails to catch the wind and move boats across the water.

The first sails were square or rectangular. Later, Arab sailors invented triangular sails that used the wind better.

Capturing the Wind

Vertical Axis Wind Turbine

Of all the Sun's energy that reaches the Earth, just 2 per cent is changed into wind – but this is still a huge amount of energy. Modern turbines capture wind using propeller-like rotor blades. These are mounted on tall towers as there is less turbulence off the ground.

Wind turbines range in size from microturbines that produce tens of watts of power to very large turbines producing millions of watts (megawatts). Turbines come in two basic shapes: horizontal axis (upright like a traditional windmill), and vertical axis (where the turbine spins around like a top).

◖ How Powerful?

The power of a wind turbine depends on the size of the rotor blades and the speed of the wind. Bigger blades and stronger winds produce more power. A 2.5 MW turbine can generate 6.5 million units of electricity each year, enough to power over 1,400 homes, make 230 million cups of tea or run a computer for 2,250 years.

◉ How a Generator Works

In 1831, British Scientist Michael Faraday discovered that electricity can be created by moving copper wire inside a magnetic field. In a wind turbine, the spinning rotor blades turn a shaft connected to the generator. The shaft makes a big coil of wire move inside a magnet. The electricity created is then carried by cables to a local network or the national grid.

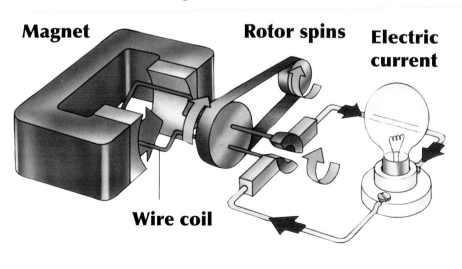

Magnet   **Rotor spins**   **Electric current**

Wire coil

▷ How Rotor Blades Work

A wind turbine's blade works like an aeroplane wing. When the wind blows, a pocket of low-pressure air forms on the downwind side of the blade. This air pocket then pulls the blade towards it. This force is called lift.

This force is much stronger than the wind's force against the front of the blade. It causes the rotor to spin around.

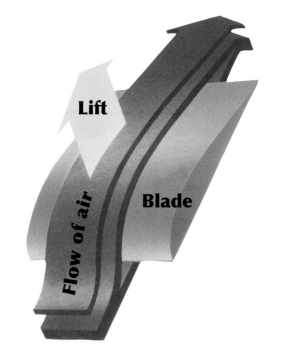

Horizontal Axis Wind Turbines (HAWTs)

Types of Turbine

Most modern turbines have blades that face the wind and turn a shaft that is parallel to the ground, like a windmill. These are known as Horizontal Axis Wind Turbines (HAWTs). In Vertical Axis Wind Turbines (VAWTs), the main shaft stands upright and the turbine spins around like a top. The most advanced VAWT is the Darrieus, named after its inventor. It has four blades that spin around very fast. It looks like a giant eggbeater.

♥ Darrieus Wind Turbine

Its shape can adjust depending on the speed of the wind.

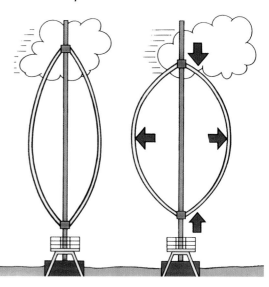

Gentle wind   Strong wind

ENERGY FACTS: HAWTs vs VAWTs

HAWTs are the most efficient wind turbine. However, tall HAWTs can be tricky to install as they need large cranes and skilled operators. They are also expensive to transport.

VAWTs such as Darrieus turbines do not need a tall tower, but it takes a strong wind to get them moving. VAWTs don't need to be turned to face the wind, but most aren't as efficient at generating electricity as HAWTs.

Wind Turbines

Modern wind turbines have come a long way since the early windmills. The rotor blades are connected to a nacelle, or casing, which sits on top of a tower. Most modern turbines have three blades. These are made from modern materials such as carbon fibre, polyester and glass fibre that allow the blade to bend without breaking. They are shaped like an aircraft wing to help them catch the wind.

The steel tower is made in sections which are lifted in place by cranes and then bolted together. Inside the nacelle are the generator, the gearbox and the electronics that control the turbine.

ENERGY FACTS: Blades

- Most turbines only have two or three blades – if they had more, the force from a strong wind might tear off the rotor.
- The blades of a wind turbine spin around between 10 and 22 times each minute. The tips can travel at speeds of over 300 km/h.
- The blades of the world's largest turbine, the E-126, are 80 metres long and stand on a tower 138 metres high.

▼ Nacelle

These engineers have opened up the hatch to the nacelle while they service a wind turbine.

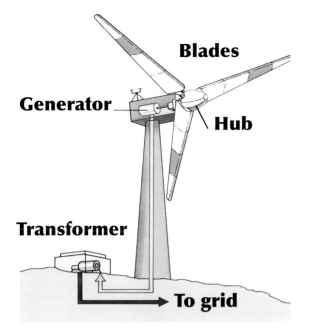

Blades

Generator

Hub

Transformer

To grid

🌀 How a Turbine Works

• The turbine blades capture wind energy and start moving. The blades are joined to the hub.

• The hub turns a slow-spinning shaft.

• The shaft is connected to a gearbox that makes another shaft, the output shaft, spin much faster.

• The output shaft is connected to a generator that turns the spinning energy into electricity, using electromagnets (see page 8).

• Electricity flows down heavy electric cables to a transformer, which is connected to the power grid.

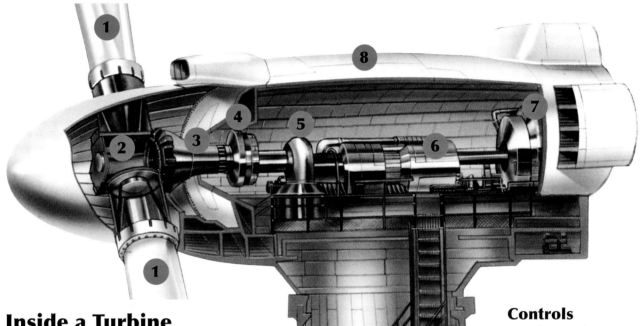

◗ Inside a Turbine

1 Blades – capture wind's energy

2 Rotor hub – controls angle of blades

3 Shaft – transfers spinning energy of rotor to generator

4 Brake – halts shaft in emergency

5 Gearbox – increases speed of shaft between rotor hub and generator

6 Generator – uses spinning energy of shaft to generate electricity

7 Controller – monitors system and ensures turbine faces the wind

8 Nacelle – main body of turbine

9 Tower – lifts blades off ground and supports rotor and nacelle

Controls

Inside a turbine an electronic controller checks the position of the wind several times per second, then moves the turbine so it is in the best position to catch the wind.

If a turbine kept turning around and around in the same direction, the cables inside could get twisted. But another controller inside untwists the cables!

Wind Farms

ENERGY FACTS: The Right Location

• The wind speed is very important: twice the speed gives eight times the power.
• Most wind turbines work in speeds of 18-90 km/h. If the wind is too slow, the blades will not turn. If it's too fast, the controller shuts down the turbine.
• When deciding on a good location, scientists test the wind speed over a long period of time with a device called an anemometer.

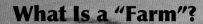

More than half of the wind energy hitting a modern turbine can be converted into electricity – but only if the turbine is in the right place. The best locations are those with regular wind and no obstacles to block the wind. As a result, many wind turbines are placed on hills or cliffs. Large wind farms are also built offshore, where the wind is stronger and more reliable, such as the 54-turbine Lynn and Inner Dowsing farm off the coast of Lincolnshire, UK.

⊽ Hill farm

This Italian wind farm is built along the crest of a hill.

What Is a "Farm"?

Wind turbines are often placed in groups in places where there are strong, steady winds all year around. These groups are called wind farms. They often stand in rows so they do not block the wind from each other.

Close to Town

The 140-turbine Whitelee wind farm in Scotland supplies 322 MW of electricity, enough to power 180,000 homes. Just 15 km from Glasgow, it is one of the first large-scale wind farms to be built close to a UK city.

⟩ Offshore Farms

There is more wind energy at sea than on land so many wind farms are built offshore. There are also few obstacles at sea so the wind is smoother and less turbulent than on land. The electricity offshore turbines generate is carried to shore along underwater cables.

Offshore turbines are harder to build, however. Calm weather is needed and only shallow coastal waters are suitable. There's also a potential danger to shipping.

⟩ Horns Rev

Built in 2002, this large wind farm off the coast of Denmark has 80 turbines, each 70 metres tall.

⟩ Building at Sea
1 *Sonar is used to position steel piles on the sea bed.*
2 *Steel piles are driven into the sea bed. They are then coated with special resins to avoid rust.*
3 *The tower is put in place.*
4 *The nacelle and rotor blades are added (right).*
5 *A ship lays cables to carry the electricity to shore.*

Local Wind Power

Smaller wind turbines can be used to power schools, farms, telephone masts, telephone boxes and railway signals. Wind power is especially useful in remote areas that are far from other power sources.

Small-scale turbines are now used across the world. Once installed, these turbines need little maintenance and will last many years. They are often used with other renewable power sources such as solar panels that convert the Sun's light into electricity.

◖ Microturbines

Very small turbines are often used on caravans and boats to charge batteries and provide electrical power. They are less noisy and produce less pollution than diesel or petrol generators.

They are more expensive per kilowatt than larger turbines, however, and the need for batteries adds to their cost.

Community wind farm

Micro-turbine

Eco-school

Homes

Power station

◖ Connecting to the Grid

In the past, most national electricity grids were based around large power stations running on fossil or nuclear fuels. Many countries are now changing their national grid to allow local wind and other renewable energy sources to sell on the extra electricity they produce on windy days or at night. Connecting to the grid avoids needing batteries to store the electricity that is produced.

 Ecoschools

Ecoschools try to live in a way that protects the environment as much as possible. They prefer renewable energy such as wind power rather than using electricity from a coal-fired power station which pollutes the air. If they produce more power than they need, in some countries they can make money by selling extra electricity back to the grid, known as "net metering".

Ecoschool

On the Farm

Medium-sized wind turbines work well on a farm, both for pumping water and for generating electricity. They range in size from 60 kW to 300 kW. A large part of the wind-generated electricity in Denmark, the Netherlands and Germany is produced by wind turbines in small clusters owned by farmers, small businesses and local communities.

Urban Turbines

A British company, Quiet Revolution, has designed a VAWT for schools and businesses that has an elegant helical, or twisted, shape. The S-shaped blades catch the wind whatever the wind direction.

This turbine is suited to towns where the wind is slower and often changes direction because of the many buildings.

Farm turbines

Small but Efficient

One of the big advantages of a local power supply is the fact that there is no need for expensive pylons and long cables to transfer electricity from a power station far away. The energy can be stored in batteries when the wind is not blowing. Small wind systems are spreading quickly; one day all of us may have a wind turbine in our garden or on top of our apartment block.

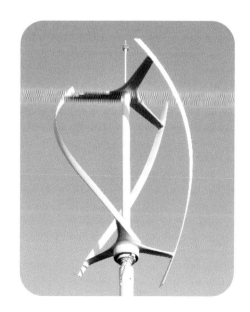

Who Uses Wind Power?

Over 50 countries around the world use wind power to generate electricity, though over 50 per cent of the total wind power generated is produced in Europe. There are wind farms in tropical regions as well as in icy arctic regions.

Wind power is one of fastest growing types of energy, having doubled in the three years between 2005 and 2008. The wind industry plans to produce 12 per cent of the world's electricity by 2020.

▷ **Lillgrund offshore wind farm** *supplies 60,000 Swedish homes.*

North and South America

Wind power is growing rapidly in the United States, which now produces more electricity from wind power than any other country. The largest wind projects are currently in Texas, the Great Plains and California.

In South America, Chile is planning the world's largest wind farm, which will produce 500 MW of electricity, while Argentina hopes to build large wind farms in the Rio Negro region.

Europe

With its many coastlines, Europe is a good place for wind power. It provides some 20 per cent of electricity in Denmark and Spain, and 10 per cent in Portugal.

The European Union plans to upgrade its power grids to allow more wind power, in an effort to reduce its emissions of the greenhouse gas, carbon dioxide.

A Home for Shellfish

Since the 1990s, many European wind farms have often been placed offshore. Underwater foundations act as a reef, encouraging the growth of mussels and other marine animals.

China

China is rapidly developing large wind farms as well as over 100,000 small 10 kW turbines in Mongolia. Today, it's easy to find Chinese herdsmen whose wind-powered tents have small washing machines and TV sets. Twice a year they pack up their belongings, including the turbine, and move to new pastures.

Developing Countries

Many developing countries, such as India, are using small 20 kW turbines to bring electricity to villages far from the electricity grid, such as Jengging village in the foothills of the Himalaya Mountains. In Morocco, 10 kW wind turbines are used to provide power to pump water from underground wells in dry areas.

Palm Springs, California, USA

ENERGY FACTS:

Worldwide Wind Power

• At the end of 2008, wind-powered generators produced 121,000 MW worldwide. That's about 1.5% of global electricity use.

• Europe took the lead in developing wind power. The five leading producers of wind power are now the United States, Germany, Spain, China and India (see map on page 31).

• Other countries developing wind power at a fast rate are Bulgaria, Australia, Poland, Turkey and Ireland.

• 440,000 people are employed in the global wind industry.

• Only 1 per cent of wind farms are placed offshore, most in Europe.

A Green Energy Source

Wind is a free source of energy. Once built, wind turbines provide clean energy with no pollution, offering a serious alternative to fossil fuels at a time when there are growing problems caused by global warming.

Wind is renewable, which means it will never run out. That said, many wind turbines may not last longer than 20 years due to wear and tear. However, the energy used to build, install, and take down a wind turbine when it no longer works is usually earned back within 3 months of operation.

◑ Roof-top Turbines

Wind turbines are now being used to provide power for office buildings.

Clean Energy

Wind energy doesn't pollute the air like the power plants that burn fossil fuels. These release the gas carbon dioxide into the atmosphere, which soaks up and traps heat from the Sun. Known as the "greenhouse effect", this is causing global warming. Burning fossil fuels also gives off harmful gases such as sulphur dioxide that cause acid rain. The only greenhouse gases created by wind power are those from the fossil fuels used to build and transport turbines.

Safe

Wind energy is safe, if turbines are put in a sensible place and serviced regularly. Onboard controls shut them down in high winds.

Tough Technology

Wind power can be used in remote regions where other types of energy are not easily available. In 2007, Scottish company Proven Energy supplied eight wind turbines to help power Belgium's Princess Elisabeth Antarctic research station near the South Pole. Wind turbines have also weathered ice storms in Slovenia, sand storms in Saudi Arabia and typhoons in Japan!

Rural Sites

Wind turbines can be built on farms or on the coast in rural areas, where many of the best wind sites are found.

Farmers can continue to work the land because the tall wind turbines use only a small part of the land.

Oil Rig ◗

Small turbines and solar panels provide power for this remote oil rig.

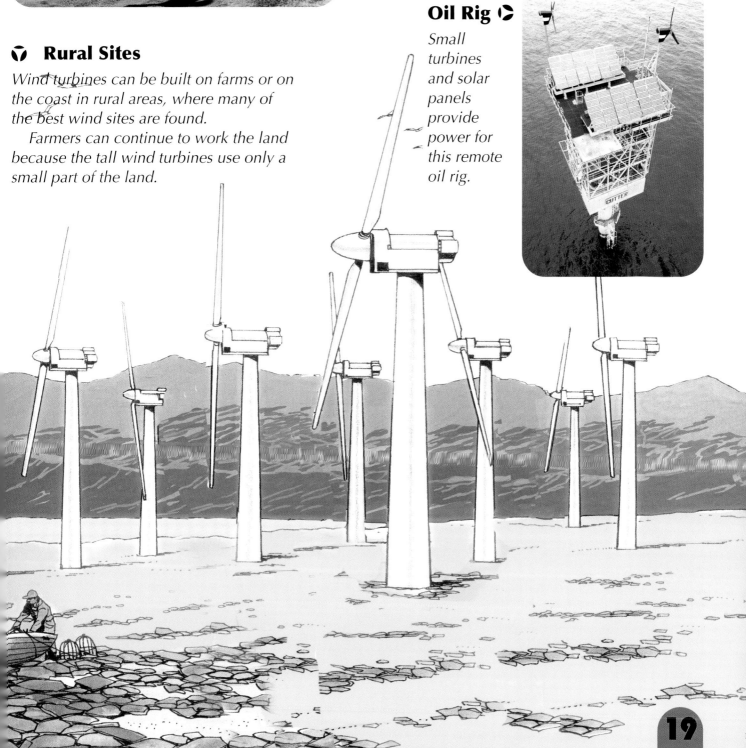

What's the Catch?

No Wind!

In recent years, wind power has become cheaper while oil and gas are likely to get more expensive. Yet one big problem remains: the wind doesn't always blow (left) when power is needed. Also, good wind sites are often located in remote locations, far from cities where the electricity is used. Wind farms can be noisy, and some people think that wind turbines are ugly. Birds have been killed by flying into the blades. However, many of these problems are being solved by new technology or by putting wind plants in suitable locations.

Space Issues

One large coal-fired power station can produce up to 5,000 megawatts, the same as 2,000 2.5 MW wind turbines, which would cover a huge area. However, while the first wind farms looked very cluttered (see below), today's turbines are larger and are spaced further apart.

Noisy Neighbours?

Turbines cause noise in two ways: the gearbox inside and air passing the blades. Some people complain this "swooshing" sound is disturbing, though most wind farms are built at least 300 metres from homes and make no more noise than a distant car engine. Modern wind turbines are quieter – you can hold a conversation directly underneath them without raising your voice.

Valley of Death?
Scientists estimate the 4,900 small turbines grouped at Altamont Pass, California, USA, kill some 4,700 birds every year, including 70 golden eagles.

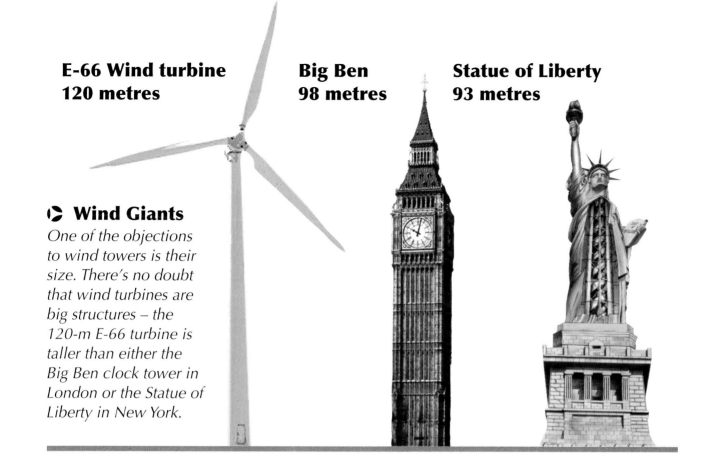

**E-66 Wind turbine
120 metres**

**Big Ben
98 metres**

**Statue of Liberty
93 metres**

◖> Wind Giants

One of the objections to wind towers is their size. There's no doubt that wind turbines are big structures – the 120-m E-66 turbine is taller than either the Big Ben clock tower in London or the Statue of Liberty in New York.

◖> A Danger to Wildlife?

Some studies suggest that large birds such as eagles are being killed when they fly into the giant turbines. In Florida, researchers are also experimenting with painting the blades with black and orange stripes to make them more visible to birds. However, it's worth remembering that pet cats kill an estimated 100 million birds each year in the United States alone.

ENERGY FACTS:
Are All Turbines White?

• Turbines are usually white or grey to fit in with usual weather conditions. But the main research into what colour would be best for turbines was carried out in Scandinavia, where it's often cloudy!

• In the USA, the Federal Aviation Administration (FAA) requires structures over 150 metres (500 feet) to be painted orange or white.

Can Wind Work?

☯ Giant Turbines

Wind turbines are getting bigger: this giant produces 5 MW compared to the 1.8 MW turbines common today.

We can expect to see more wind farms and more powerful turbines. In 100 years' time, wind power could be a very important source of energy, perhaps combined with solar power and fuel cells. As it becomes easier to sell electricity to the grid, people are more likely to build small and medium-sized turbines to power local farms, businesses and homes.

But how reliable is wind power – can electricity be stored for those times when the wind isn't blowing? Proposed solutions include fuel cells, compressed air and linked power grids so that even if it's calm where you live, turbines are creating electricity for your home hundreds of kilometres away.

◐ Charging Electric Cars

Denmark gets about 20 per cent of its electrical power from wind. On windy days, that percentage can double. There are plans to build a nationwide system to charge electric cars with the surplus wind power, with charging spots (see right) and battery-exchange locations across Denmark.

1 *Hydrogen flows into fuel cell.*

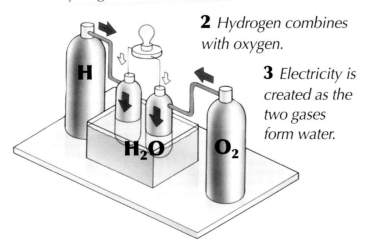

2 *Hydrogen combines with oxygen.*

3 *Electricity is created as the two gases form water.*

◑ Fuel Cells

One way to store the electricity generated by wind turbines is to use it to make hydrogen. A fuel cell combines hydrogen and oxygen to produce electricity, heat and water.

This electricity can be used to power an electric car or fed into the grid during peak hours. A fuel cell doesn't lose its charge – it continues to produce electricity as long as hydrogen is supplied.

Fuel cells have no major moving parts, so they are also very reliable, one reason why they are used to power space shuttles far out in space.

Floating Turbines

The proposed SWAY system from Norway is a floating foundation capable of supporting a 5 MW wind turbine in water depths from 80m to more than 300m. It can work in some of the world's roughest offshore locations.

Due to higher average wind speeds out to sea, floating turbines may produce 30 per cent more electricty that those closer to shore.

◗ Compressed Air Storage

"Dispatchable" wind turbines convert wind energy into stored energy, by using a compressor inside turbines (1) to pump air along steel pipes (2) into storage tanks (3). When power is needed, generators (4) use the compressed air to create electricity or drive machinery. The electricity can be used to supply the grid (5) during peak hours.

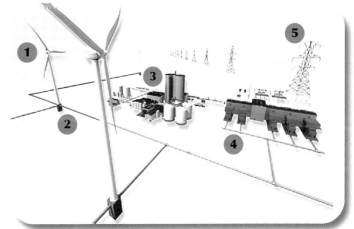

Future Trends

Scientists are looking at ways of improving wind turbines, such as nodding turbines that can deal with strong gusts of wind. More ambitious projects include offshore turbines on rafts, kite turbines such as the laddermill, and balloon windmills that generate electricity high in the sky.

Skyscrapers are already being designed to catch wind and generate their own electricity. Wind is being used again to power ships and there are even hand-held generators that can power MP3 players and digital cameras.

🜂 Handheld Turbines

The HYmini is a handheld device that uses wind and solar power to generate electricity. It can recharge small 5-volt electronic gadgets such as mobile phones, MP3 players and digital cameras.

◖ Tower Turbines

The sail-shaped towers of the Bahrain Trade Centre are joined by three 29-metre wind turbines. They deliver up to 15 per cent of the building's power. The shape of each tower has been designed so that wind hitting it is directed onto the turbines.

ENERGY FACTS: Wind in the UK

• The first wind farm in the UK was built at Delabole in 1991, which had 10 wind turbines.
• By September 2009, the UK was home to 248 wind farms and 2,636 wind turbines. These can produce almost 3,831 MW of power, enough to power over 2 million homes.
• The UK has the best potential in Europe for generating power from wind.

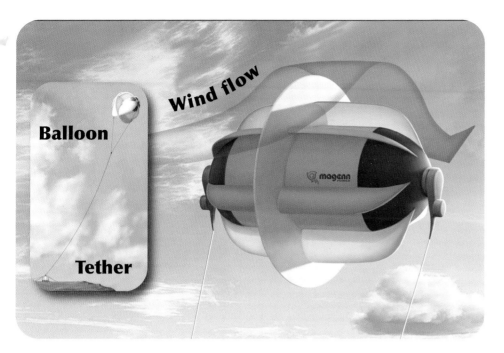

Balloon

Wind flow

Tether

◁ Balloon Turbines

The Magenn Air Rotor System, or MARS, is a balloon that creates electricity. Once the balloon rises to between 100 and 300 metres, where the wind runs strong and steady, the MARS starts spinning and generating electricity. This travels through cables to the ground to a set of batteries for later use, or to the power grid.

▷ Laddermill

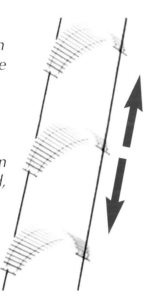

A Laddermill is a design for a wind turbine made up of a long string of power kites that would reach a height of about 9,000 metres. The kites pull on the long rope on which they are tethered, and the energy is then used to drive an electric generator.

▷ Kite Sails

A German company, SkySails, is developing large kites that fly 400 m above ships. These cut down the amount of diesel the ships use by using wind power to pull them along. The automated kite launches from a ship's bow (front) and sails to a height of 100 to 400 metres to help propel the vessel.

SkySails claims that its kites could cut the amount of fuel that a ship uses by 10 to 35 per cent a year.

HOT OFF THE PRESS

New spin on an old idea

■ Ancient Persian buildings used air currents and reservoirs of water to keep cool. A new roof-top turbine has been inspired by these "wind catchers". It is called the Windation.

Wind blows in the top and is directed to the bottom where the wind turns a turbine that can generate up to 5 kilowatts of electricity.

The units work well with what's called "dirty wind" – the gusty, inconsistent wind often found in urban areas where buildings break up the flow of wind.

The Windation – as the moving parts are enclosed, there is less danger to birds.

New record for wind power

■ Spain, which along with Germany and Denmark is among the three biggest producers of wind power in the EU, aims to triple the amount of energy it gets from renewable sources by 2020.

One week in November 2008, Spain's wind turbines produced some 10,000 MW of power – or nearly 43% of the total country's demand for electricity. Though this may have been a week when demand was low, it shows how wind power has the potential to provide a large part of our energy needs.

The robot inspector

■ Until now, humans have inspected wind turbines. It can be a tricky job examining a 60-m long rotor blade high off the ground. Now German scientists have come up with the RIWEA, a robot detective.

The robot pulls itself up a rope until it reaches the rotor blades. Then it goes to work, inspecting every part of a rotor blade with a variety of cameras and heat sensors that look for cracks and examine joints. If any cracks or faults are found, the robot records the damage and exactly where it is.

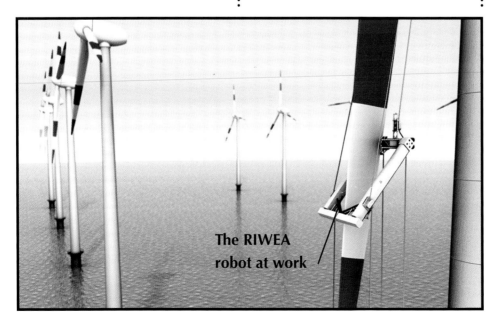

The RIWEA robot at work

Wind + Water working together

A Scottish firm has come up with a great idea for combining wind and water energy. Their Wave Treader machines can be mounted on the base of offshore wind turbines. In the right weather, each machine could generate almost half a megawatt, enough to power 125 homes.

How does it work? As waves ripple past the wave power machine, they move arms either side of the turbine in turn. These push against cylinders that contain hydraulic fluid. These spin a hydraulic motor which in turn drives an electricity generator. The electricity is then transmitted back to shore along the cable shared with the wind turbine.

A Wave Treader turns to face the waves, so it works whatever direction the waves are moving.

Wave Treaders hook a wave machine up to a wind turbine.

Doughnut power?

The Wind Energiser is a large plastic and steel funnel that directs wind at the rotor blades of wind turbines. The funnel's manufacturers claim that their doughnut-shaped structure could increase the efficiency of a wind turbine by up to 30 per cent and reduce the strain on the rotor blades by providing a more balanced flow of air.

> " Adding wind turbines to pylons and towers could solve the problem of where to put new turbines.

Making use of pylons and towers

The winners of the 2009 Next Generation design competition came up with a clever yet simple idea – adding wind turbines to already existing electrical towers.

The project, called Wind-It, shows how wind turbines can be built on pylons and towers along high voltage lines across the United States. A single turbine could generate up to a megawatt of power.

How the wind turbines might look inside a pylon

How Wind Compares

While fossil fuels are cheap, they release carbon dioxide into the atmosphere, causing pollution and global warming. Wind power and other forms of renewable energy will reduce this problem, but may only be able to supply 20 per cent of our energy needs. Nuclear power could provide us with the extra power, but reactors are very expensive and take years to build.

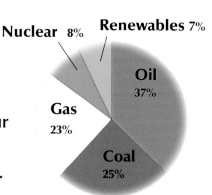

World Energy Sources

Nuclear 8%
Renewables 7%
Oil 37%
Gas 23%
Coal 25%

NON-RENEWABLE ENERGY

Oil

For:
Oil is cheap and easy to store, transport and use.

Against:
Oil is not renewable and it is getting more expensive to get out of the ground. Burning oil releases large amounts of greenhouse gases. Oil spills, especially at sea, cause severe pollution.

Gas

For:
Gas is relatively cheap, and produces less greenhouses gases than oil and coal.

Against:
Burning gas releases carbon dioxide. Gas is not renewable and the world's natural gas reserves are limited. Gas pipelines can disrupt the migration routes of animals such as caribou.

Coal

For:
Coal is cheap and supplies of coal are expected to last another 150 years.

Against:
Coal-fired power stations give off the most greenhouse gases. They also produce sulphur dioxide, creating acid rain. Coal mining can be very destructive to the landscape.

Nuclear

For:
Nuclear power is constant and reliable, and doesn't contribute to global warming.

Against:
Not renewable as uranium (the main nuclear fuel) will eventually run out. Nuclear waste is so dangerous it must be buried for thousands of years. Also the risk of a nuclear accident.

RENEWABLE ENERGY

Wind Power

For:

Wind power needs no fuel, it's renewable and doesn't pollute.

Against:

Wind is unpredictable, so wind farms need a back-up power supply. Possible danger to bird flocks. It takes thousands of wind turbines to produce the same power as a nuclear plant.

Solar Power

For:

Solar power needs no fuel, it's renewable and doesn't pollute.

Against:

Solar power stations are very expensive as solar (photovoltaic) cells cost a lot compared to the amount of electricity they produce. They're unreliable unless used in a very sunny climate.

Hydroelectric Power

For:

Hydroelectric power needs no fuel, is renewable and doesn't pollute.

Against:

Hydroelectric power is very expensive to build. A large dam will flood a very large area upstream, impacting on animals and people there. A dam can affect water quality downstream.

Geothermal Power

For:

Geothermal power needs no fuel, it's renewable and doesn't pollute.

Against:

There aren't many suitable places for a geothermal power station as you need hot rocks of the right type and not too deep. It can "run out of steam". Underground poisonous gases can be a danger.

Biofuels

For:

Biofuels are cheap and renewable and can be made from waste.

Against:

Growing biofuels from energy crops reduces the land available for food and uses up vital resources such as fresh water. Like fossil fuels, biofuels can produce greenhouse gases.

Tidal Power

For:

Tidal power needs no fuel, is reliable, renewable and doesn't pollute.

Against:

Tidal power machines are expensive to build and only provide power for around 10 hours each day, when the tide is actually moving in or out. Not an efficient way of producing electricity.

Glossary and Resources

anemometer An instrument that measures the speed of the wind.

atmosphere The thick blanket of air that surrounds the Earth.

blade A long, flat surface, shaped like an aircraft wing, that captures the wind's energy. Most modern wind turbines have two or three blades.

climate The average weather in a region over a long period of time.

compressor A device that increases the pressure of a gas by compressing it (squeezing it into a smaller space).

controller A computer that monitors a wind turbine, making sure it lines up with the wind.

fantail The small wheel at the back of a windmill that turns the main sails to face into the wind.

fossil fuel A fuel such as coal, oil or gas that was formed underground from the remains of prehistoric plants and animals.

fuel cell A device that combines hydrogen and oxygen to create electricity that can be used to power an electric car.

generator A machine that turns mechanical energy into electrical energy.

global warming A warming of the Earth's surface. Many scientists predict that global warming may lead to more floods, droughts and rising sea levels.

greenhouse effect The global warming caused by human-made gases, such as carbon dioxide and methane, that trap the heat from the Sun in the atmosphere.

megawatt (MW) A million watts (a watt is a unit of power). A gigawatt is 1,000 MW.

nacelle The part of a wind turbine that contains the gears and generator.

power station A plant where electricity is generated.

pylon A tall metal tower that supports high voltage electric cables.

renewable Something that can be used over and over without running out.

rotor The spinning mechanism on a turbine that includes the blades.

sail Any surface that captures the wind's power and turns it into movement.

shaft A rod that transfers the spinning energy of the rotor to the generator.

trade winds Steady winds blowing from east to west above and below the equator. They got their name as merchants long ago relied on them to make long sea voyages.

turbine A machine with rotating blades.

wind farm A group of wind turbines placed together in a windy location.

wind pump A wind machine that pumps water from deep underground.

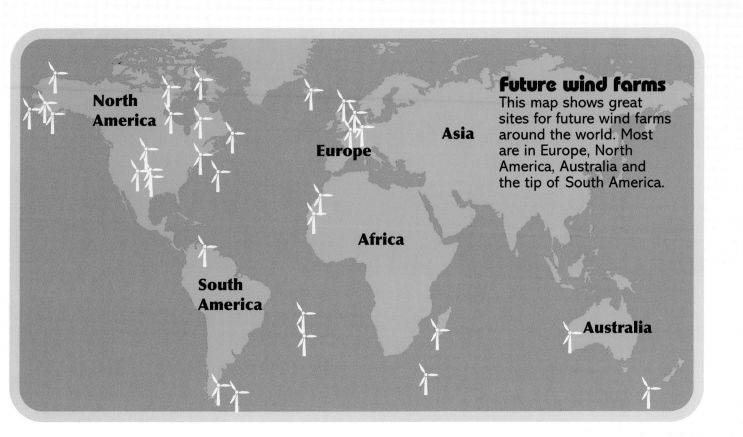

Future wind farms

This map shows great sites for future wind farms around the world. Most are in Europe, North America, Australia and the tip of South America.

North America

Europe

Asia

Africa

South America

Australia

Useful Websites

If you're interested in finding out more about wind power, the following websites are helpful:

www.therenewableenergycentre.co.uk
www.embracewind.com
www.provenenergy.co.uk
www.wwindea.org
www.awea.org
www.auswind.org
www.windenergy.org.nz

ENERGY FACTS:
Top Ten Wind Power Nations

The ten countries with the most wind power in 2008 were (power given in megawatts):

1 **United States** – 25,170 MW
2 **Germany** – 23,903 MW
3 **Spain** – 16,740 MW
4 **China** – 12,210 MW
5 **India** – 9,587 MW
6 **Italy** – 3,736 MW
7 **France** – 3,404 MW
8 **UK** – 3,288 MW
9 **Denmark** – 3,160 MW
10 **Portugal** – 2,862 MW

Further Reading

World Issues: Energy Crisis by Ewan McLeish (Aladdin/Watts)
Issues in Our World: Energy Crisis by Ewan McLeish (Aladdin/Watts)
Your Environment: Future Energy by Sally Morgan (Aladdin/Watts)
Saving Our World: New Energy Sources by Nigel Hawkes (Aladdin/Watts)
Our World: Wind Energy by Rob Bowden (Aladdin/Watts)
Energy Sources: Wind Power by Neil Morris (Franklin Watts)

Index

acid rain 18
air currents 6
air pressure 9
anemometers 12, 30
atmosphere 7, 30

batteries 14, 15
blades 4, 9, 10, 11, 30

cliffs 7
climate 30
coastline 5, 19
community wind
  farms 14, 15
compressed air
  storage 23
controllers 11, 18, 30

danger to wildlife 5,
  20, 21

ecoschools 15
electric cars 22
electricity 3, 8, 11,
  13, 22, 25

fantails 4, 30
farms 5, 15, 19
fossil fuels 3, 5, 18,
  20, 28, 30
fuel cells 22, 30

future 22-23, 24-25,
  26-27

gears 4, 11
generators 8, 11, 30
global warming 3,
  18, 30
greenhouse gases 5,
  18, 30

history 5
hub 11
hydrogen 22

jetstream 7

kites 7, 25
  Laddermill 25

marine animals 17
megawatts 8, 30
microturbines 14

nacelles 10, 11, 30
NASA (North American
  Space Agency) 22
net metering 15
noise 5, 20
nuclear power 28

oil rigs 19

power grid 11, 14, 15
power stations 3, 14,
  15, 20, 30
pros and cons 5,
  28, 29
pylons 27, 30

reliability 5, 18
renewable energy
  sources 18-19, 29, 30
robots 26
rotors 9, 30

safety 18
sails 5, 7, 25, 30
shafts 11, 30
ships 25
skyscrapers 24
Sun 6, 8, 18

towers 10, 11, 12
transformers 11

wave power 27
wear and tear 18
weather 6, 13
wind 6-7
  direction 11
  energy 6-7
  speed 12, 23
  world 6

wind farms 5, 12-13, 30
  Altamont Pass 20
  building 12
  Horns Rev 13
  Lillgrund 16-17
  Palm Springs 16-17
  UK 24
  Whitelee 12
windmills 4, 5, 10
wind pumps 3, 5, 30
windsurfers 7
wind turbines 30
  Antarctic 19
  balloon 25
  buildings 15, 18, 24
  colour 21
  Darrieus 9
  floating 23
  handheld 24
  HAWTs 8-9
  how they work 11
  materials 10
  offshore 13
  power 8
  size 21, 22
  VAWTs 8-9, 15
  Windation 26
  Wind energiser 27
  Wind-It concept 27
world wind power
  16-17

Photocredits

(Abbreviations: t – top, m – middle, b – bottom, l – left, r – right).

All photos istockphoto.com except: 3b: Nordex GmbH. 10b, 16-17: Siemens press picture. 13br: courtesy AMEC. 15tr & 15br: courtesy Quiet Revolution. 18tl and 19tr: Proven Energy. 19tl: The International Polar Foundation. 20b: Michael Svoboda/dreamstime.com. 22tl: BARD Engineering GmbH/Lang. 23t: courtesy StatoilHydro. 23br: courtesy General Compression. 25tl: courtesy Magenn Power Inc. 25bl: courtesy SkySails GmbH. 26br: courtesy Fraunhofer Institute. 26t: Windation Energy Systems, Inc. 27tr: Green Ocean Energy Ltd. 27b: courtesy www.metropolismag.com.